Lucky in *Love*

Iris Howden

Published in association with
The Basic Skills Agency

Hodder & Stoughton
A MEMBER OF THE HODDER HEADLINE GROUP

Cataloguing in Publication Data is available from the British Library.

ISBN 0 340 69694 X

First published 1997
Impression number   10 9 8 7 6 5 4 3 2 1
Year   2002 2001 2000 1999 1998 1997

Typeset by Fakenham Photosetting Ltd, Fakenham, Norfolk.
Printed in Great Britain for Hodder & Stoughton Educational, a division of
Hodder Headline Plc, 338 Euston Road, London NW1 3BH by Athenaeum Press
Ltd, Gateshead, Tyne & Wear.

Lucky in Love

Contents

Bad News

The sun was in my eyes as I drove.
It was so bright I had to stop
and put on my dark glasses.
But it was not just the sunlight
bringing tears to my eyes.
It was a sad day for me.

Jamie's phone call had been a shock.
At first I couldn't take in the news.
Aunt Peg dead?

There must be some mistake.

She was always so fit and well.

The tone of his voice told me

this was for real.

'She had a heart attack,' he said.

'It was all over in seconds.'

I woke my flatmate, Kim, and told her.

'I must go to Yorkshire in the morning

to arrange the funeral.

Aunt Peg hasn't any other family.'

Then I rang my mum in San Francisco.

It was still afternoon out there.

Mum was in the States on honeymoon.

Two weeks before, she had married

Bill Davis, her boss.

Now I felt pleased that we had

all been together at the wedding.

It was the last time I had seen Aunt Peg.

It was Aunt Peg who had helped me
sort out my life after the accident.
She made me see that being in a wheelchair
needn't stop me from having a good life.
Peg showed me that my mum had her own
life to lead. I had been selfish in the past.
I didn't want to spoil Mum's chance
of happiness now. I told her I would
take care of everything.

'Are you sure, Sally?' she said.
'Can you can handle it alone?'
'I won't be alone. I've got Jamie.'
I said. 'Aunt Peg wouldn't have wanted
you to cut short your honeymoon.
And extra flights would cost a lot.
You and Bill need all your spare cash.'
They were hoping to set up a new branch
of his business in the States.

I spent the rest of the night packing.

It takes me longer than it would take

most people. People who can walk.

Kim was a great help.

She made me black coffee and wrote a list

of all that had to be done.

Even though I was upset

I couldn't wait to see Jamie again.

2

The Funeral

When Jamie came out to meet me
he looked terrible. He was pale
with dark rings under his eyes.
We kissed. He helped me unload the car.
Inside, the house was in a mess.
Aunt Peg's slippers were still on the mat.
Her coat hung from the back of a chair
– as if she might walk in any minute.
Jess, her old dog lay with her head
on her paws, not moving, missing Peg.

I looked sadly round the dusty room.

This was not the homecoming I had planned.

I had waited two years for the day

when I would come back to Yorkshire

for good. It had been my dream to run

the market garden with Peg and Jamie.

I had done well at college.

My name had been put forward

for the STUDENT OF THE YEAR award.

Now if I won it Aunt Peg wouldn't

be there to see me get the prize.

Jamie put his arms round me.

'Don't cry Sally,' he said.

I need you to be strong.'

The funeral took place two days later.

The tiny church was packed

with farmers and their wives.

And Peg's friends from the village.

Jamie and I sat in the front pew.

Light from the stained-glass windows

shone on the white-washed walls.

There were flowers everywhere.

Afterwards people came back to the house.

We poured out drinks, passed round

plates of food.

People wanted to talk about Peg.
To tell us how kind she had been.

The next day there was a lot to do.
We had to clear out Peg's clothes.
Go through the papers in her desk.
It was in a worse muddle than ever.
Jamie didn't seem to have a clue
about that side of the business.

3

Breaking Up

We went into town to see the solicitor.
To hear him read the will.
Peg had left everything she had
to be shared between Jamie and myself.
She had given Jamie a home and a job.
He had been like a son to her.

As it turned out there wasn't any money.
My aunt's business had really gone
downhill in the last year or two.

There was the cottage
but without money it would be hard
to keep the business going.

'Will your mum lend us some?' Jamie asked.
'I can't ask her at the moment,' I said.
'She and Bill need all their money
for the new business.'
'Well, that's it then,' Jamie said.
He didn't even try to borrow from the bank.
I think he was afraid of going it alone.
I was taken aback when he gave up so easily.
'Don't be so wet!' I wanted to shout
but I could see he'd made up his mind.

'We can live here,' Jamie said.
'I'll get a job. Bob Jones has asked me
to work for him.'
It seemed the best thing to do.

But I felt let down.

This wasn't how I'd seen our life together.

I stayed on for a while. I didn't enjoy it.

Jamie set off early every morning.

It was a long drive to work.

When he came home he was tired out.

All he wanted to do was sleep.

We hardly spoke.

So much seemed to have changed between us.

I moved into a separate room.

I made up my mind to go back home.

I missed Kim and my other friends.

And I wanted to get a job.

It wouldn't be easy in this area.

There wasn't much office work here.

At last Jamie said we should sell
the cottage and split the money.

He could live in at the Jones' place.

Then he wouldn't have to travel to work.

I felt hurt that he had made his plans

without asking me.

But I had to agree it made sense.

Jamie and I didn't seem so close

any more. We had grown apart.

Those two years at college

had made a big difference.

We had both changed.

We didn't have much in common now.

I had to face up to things.

I could no longer see a future

for us together.

It was time for that chapter of my life

to close. And a new one to begin.

We agreed to split up.

4

The Interview

I threw myself into finding a job.

Anything to keep myself busy.

To stop me thinking about Jamie.

I bought the newspaper every night

and read all the adverts.

I wrote dozens of letters.

Sent out copies of my CV.

And I got a few interviews.

Once or twice I might have got

the job – if I hadn't been disabled.

No-one wanted to take a chance
on someone in a wheelchair.
They didn't say that of course.

It was always 'We need someone
who has done this sort of job before,' or
'We have a lot of people to see.'

Then a job came up at Fosters.
This was a big company
that made parts for washing machines.
They employed disabled people
in their factory.
So I applied for the job of PA
to the director.
I found out all about the firm.
Read leaflets about their machines.
I drove out to see if there was
easy parking. If there was access
for a wheelchair at the entrance.

The day of the interview came
and I knew I had done well.

Old Mr Foster who owned the firm
was keen on me because I had won
the STUDENT OF THE YEAR award.
The PA who was leaving
said my shorthand and typing
speeds were good.
I could tell that the younger son,
Gavin, liked me.

The only one of the panel who didn't
seem too sure was Simon Foster.
He was Mr Foster's older son.
He would be taking over the firm
so his vote was important.
They asked me to go out of the room
while they talked it over.
At last they called me in and told me
I had got the job.

5

Working Girl

I started work the next week.

Mr Foster was a lovely old chap.

He helped me move things round

so I could turn my wheelchair

to work at the desk or at the computer.

There was a lot to learn but

he went out of his way to help me.

All the staff liked Mr Foster.

Linda, the West Indian girl

on the reception desk told me

he took on many black and Asian workers

as well as disabled people.

He even took men who had been in prison.

He told me no-one had ever let him down.

'Look at you, Sally,' he said.

You're the best PA I've ever had.'

Mr Foster's health wasn't good.

He spent more and more time at home.

When Simon took over he made changes.

He always seemed to be in a hurry.

It made me nervous so I made

one or two silly mistakes.

I could see him looking at me as if

he'd been wrong to give me the job.

He brought in a new computer.

'We need to up-date the system,' he said.

It meant a lot of extra work for me.

I spent hours typing in the data.

Bringing our records up to date.

One day I forgot to press SAVE

and lost a whole file.

Simon was angry.

'Just say if you can't manage,' he said.

'Of course I can manage,' I snapped.

'I'll stay behind and put it right.'

I took the manual home with me to read
so I wouldn't make any more mistakes.
'Take it easy,' Kim said. 'Slow down.'
'I want to make a success of this job,'
I told her. 'I can't let Mr high-and-mighty
Simon Foster think he's beaten me.'

'What about the other brother?' Kim asked.
'Gavin. What's he like?'
'He's great.' I told her. 'Really nice.
He's on the sales side so he's often out.'
It made all the difference
when Gavin was in the office.
He was easy going. And so good looking.
All the girls from the typing pool
flocked in. He made them laugh.

All except Linda.
She did her best to ignore him.

'What's the matter with Linda?'
I asked Julie. She told me
'Linda used to go out with Gavin.
I don't think Simon likes
Gavin mixing with the office girls.'
Typical of Simon, I thought.
Working girls weren't good enough
for him.

6

Having Fun

Gavin often used to stop for a chat.

He'd tease me about my wheelchair.

'How's the Ferrari?' he'd say

'Going in for the Grand Prix yet?'

I liked the way he made a joke of it.

One day he asked me out.

'You know Sally,' he said, 'you've got

beautiful eyes and a lovely smile.

But you're always so serious.

Don't you ever want to have fun?'

'Of course,' I said, 'but life hasn't been
a bundle of laughs lately.
My aunt died a short while ago
then I broke up with my boy friend ...'
I stopped. Why I was telling him all this?
Gavin was so easy to talk to.
'All the more reason to enjoy yourself,'
he said. 'Have dinner with me tonight.'

That evening was to be the first of many.
Gavin would call for me in his sports car
and whisk me off to some smart restaurant.
He knew all the latest places.
Everywhere we went people came up
to chat. He was a really popular guy.

But Kim, my flatmate didn't take to him.
'He's much too smooth,' she said.
'Oh, he's got bags of charm,

but I'd hate to see you get hurt.

Don't get too serious, Sally.'

I didn't want to listen to her.

I was having fun for the first time in ages.

Then there was Simon.

He found me working on Gavin's sales figures.

'I don't pay you to do my brother's work,'

he said in quite a nasty way.

'Excuse me, but this is my lunch hour,'
I told him sharply. He wasn't going
to stop me from seeing Gavin.
My private life was my own affair.

I also had a run in with Linda.
She waited until we were alone one day.
'I don't know how to say this Sally,'
she said. 'It's none of my business.
Be careful with Gavin. He's a playboy.
He'll only let you down.'
'Thanks for the warning,' I said.
'But I can take care of myself.
I'm not a child you know.'
Inside I was boiling.
How dare she talk down to me like that!
I told myself she was just jealous
because Gavin had dropped her.

7

The Dinner Party

We were busy at work with new orders

from abroad.

One day a customer rang from Paris.

He didn't speak any English.

Simon was out so I did my best

to talk to him. I was glad

I'd kept up with my French.

Simon was really pleased with me.

'You did very well, Sally,' he said.

'That order was worth a lot of money.'

A word of praise from Simon at last!

I hadn't seen Gavin for days.

But I was due to meet him on Saturday.

Kim was giving a dinner party then.

Saturday came. I went to get my hair done.

I wanted to show Gavin I could look good

– even if I was in a wheelchair.

When I got back there was a huge bunch

of flowers waiting for me.

'Gavin rang,' Kim told me. 'He's sorry.

He can't make it tonight.'

'Did he send these flowers?' I asked.

'No,' Kim said. 'His brother Simon

dropped by with them.'

I looked at the card fixed to them.

THANKS FOR ALL YOUR HARD WORK.

SIMON, it said.

Maybe Simon wasn't so bad after all!

'I must ring and thank him,' I said.

'No need,' Kim said. 'You'll see him later.

I've asked him to dinner in place of Gavin.

You never told me Simon was so dishy.'

I stared at her. Simon dishy!

It had not struck me that he was

even good looking!

I looked at him with new eyes that evening.

Kim had told him to wear casual clothes.

Simon looked quite different in jeans

and a sweater. Younger – and much nicer

away from the office.

Kim said that I had cooked the food.

'Is there no end to Sally's talents?'

Simon said. 'A first rate PA

and a brilliant cook as well.

She even speaks French,' he told Jack.

'Only a little,' I said.

'Enough to get us a big order,' he said.

I blushed. Praise from Simon twice

in one week was too much!

The evening was a great success.

Jack and Simon got on well,

I could see that Kim liked Simon.

'He's far better than his brother,'

she said after the men had gone.

'I don't know why

you waste your time on Gavin.

Look how he let you down tonight.'

'I don't suppose he meant to,' I said.

'He had to go away on business.'

'Did he?' Kim said. 'While you were

making the coffee Simon let it slip

that he didn't know where his brother was.

Gavin had just taken a few days off.

It's not the first time he's done it.'

I didn't say anything.

Simon could take care of himself.

But he had looked very tired lately.

It must be a strain running the firm.

I was glad I'd been there for him.

8

Seeing Clearly

On Monday Simon thanked me for the meal.
'I like your friends very much,' he said.
'Yes,' I said. 'They're great ...'
I broke off as Gavin came in, all smiles,
– as if nothing had happened.
Simon gave him a funny look
and took him into his office.
I could hear their raised voices.

Then Gavin came out looking angry.

'My brother,' he said.

'Treats me like a kid.'

'Never mind,' I said. 'Cheer up.

We're going away this weekend.

Or had you forgotten?'

We had fixed it weeks ago.

'Of course not,' Gavin said.

'I'll pick you up on Friday.'

'Are you sure this is a good idea?'

Kim asked as she helped me pack.

'You going sailing?'

'I've got to try it,' I told her.

'You never know. I might love it.'

I didn't though. I hated it.

The whole weekend was awful.

When we got to the hotel I found

Gavin had booked a double room,

on the second floor.
'There's been a mistake,'
I told the reception clerk,
'Could you give me a single one
on the ground floor?'

Gavin tried to make a joke of it
but I couldn't see the funny side.
'Didn't you check with the hotel?'
I said. 'To ask if there was a lift?
And what made you think I'd want to
share a room?'

Things went from bad to worse after that.
I hated being on Gavin's boat.
I couldn't move about at all
so I soon got cold and wet.
When we got back to the hotel
I said I wanted an early night.

'I told my friends we'd meet them
later for a drink,' Gavin said.
'You go,' I said. 'I'll be fine.'

The next day he went sailing with them.
I wasn't going to risk it again.
I spent a lonely day.
It was only a tiny seaside place.
There wasn't much to do.
I looked at the gulls, the boats
in the harbour and the pier.
There were a few wooden stalls
selling seafood or rock.
Buckets and spades for the children.

There was one hut with a notice that said
MADAME OLGA
GYPSY FORTUNE TELLER

LEARN WHAT THE FUTURE
HOLDS FOR YOU.
I went inside to pass the time.
Madame Olga looked a bit like Mavis,
the cleaning lady at our office.
All she needed was a cigarette
hanging from the corner of her mouth.
She looked bored but woke up a bit
at the sight of my five pound note.
She went to work reading my palm.

It was short and sweet.
'You've had your troubles,' she said.
'But things will change for the better.
I see long life and happiness ahead.
And you'll be lucky in love.'

'What rubbish!' I told myself later
as I sat drinking tea in a seedy cafe.

I hadn't been lucky in love so far.

My first boy friend, Rob, had left me

after the accident. He couldn't handle

the fact that I would never walk again.

Jamie had turned out to be weak.

He needed someone to take care of him.

As for Gavin! I had been crazy to think
he would be the third man in my life.

I didn't blame him for getting bored
with me. It couldn't be much fun dating
a girl in a wheelchair.
But he was so selfish! Fancy leaving me
all alone in a strange place.
There was worse to come.
Gavin didn't appear at dinner time.
Next morning there was no sign of him.
He'd left me a note. It said:
HAVE GONE WITH SOME OF THE LADS
ACROSS THE CHANNEL FOR A FEW
DAYS. CAN YOU MAKE
YOUR OWN WAY BACK? GAVIN.

9

Help is at Hand

I could not believe my eyes!

This was the end.

How on earth was I to get home?

My own car is specially fitted out

so I can drive. I had come in Gavin's.

There was no way

I could travel by bus or train.

I rang Kim to ask her to fetch me.

But there was no reply. She was out.

There was only one other person

I could ask for help.

Simon arrived at lunchtime.
He must have driven very fast
to get there so soon.
He rushed into the hotel
and put his arms round me.
'Are you all right, Sally?'
He looked really worried.
'Of course,' I said. 'I'm sorry to drag
you down here but I didn't know
how I was going to get home.'

'I could kill my brother,' Simon said
when I told him what had happened.
'What a terrible way to treat you.
But that's Gavin for you.
Our mother spoiled him.
He always does exactly what he wants.

He's like a child. He uses people.

I'm afraid he treats women very badly.

He gave poor Linda a hard time.

That's why I don't like him going out

with girls from the office.'

I went red thinking of how I had spoken

to Linda. How I had snapped at Simon

when he had tried to stop me doing

Gavin's work. I could see now

they had been trying to protect me.

'Are you sure you're OK?' Simon asked.

'I'm fine,' I said. 'But

I'll soon need a lot more help.

I don't know how I'll cope alone

when Kim and Jack get married.'

'You won't be alone,' Simon said.

'I'll always be here for you.

Do you know, Sally, that's the first time
I've every heard you admit
you need other people.
You bit my head off when I wanted to
show you how the new computer worked.'
I stared at him. A lot of things
started to make sense. I had let
my pride get in the way then too.
Simon had only been trying to help me!

He went back to the subject of Gavin.
'I'll be glad when he leaves,' he said.
'Leaves?' I asked. 'Where's he going?'
'To Australia,' Simon said. 'I'm buying
his share of the business.
Hasn't he said anything to you?'
'Not a word,' I said. 'What will you do?
Look for a new partner?'

'I've got one in mind,' Simon said,
smiling at me. 'How about it Sally?
We'd make a good team. What do you say?'
'I haven't much money to invest,' I said.
'You won't need any,' Simon said.
'I'm asking you to marry me.'

10

Happiness

I didn't say yes there and then.

I needed time to think about it.

To sort out my feelings.

But looking back that was the day

when I began to realise

that Simon was the one for me.

Kim was over the moon when I told her.

'What did I tell you?' she said.

'Simon's twice the man Gavin is.

I'm so happy for you Sally.
Just think, this time next year
we could both be married.'

Simon and I have been together
for a year now.
He's everything I could wish for
in a husband. He's kind and caring.
My best friend as well as my
business partner.
So Madame Olga's fortune telling
came true after all.
I don't know if I'll have a long life
but it's turned out to be a happy one.
At last I've been lucky in love.